The Masked Cleaning Ladies of Om

JOHN COLDWELL

Illustrated by Joseph Sharples

OXFORD
UNIVERSITY PRESS

OXFORD

UNIVERSITY PRESS

Great Clarendon Street, Oxford OX2 6DP

Oxford University Press is a department of the University of Oxford.
It furthers the University's objective of excellence in research, scholarship,
and education by publishing worldwide in

Oxford   New York

Auckland   Cape Town   Dar es Salaam   Hong Kong   Karachi
Kuala Lumpur   Madrid   Melbourne   Mexico City   Nairobi
New Delhi   Shanghai   Taipei   Toronto

With offices in

Argentina   Austria   Brazil   Chile   Czech Republic   France   Greece
Guatemala   Hungary   Italy   Japan   Poland   Portugal   Singapore
South Korea   Switzerland   Thailand   Turkey   Ukraine   Vietnam

Oxford is a registered trade mark of Oxford University Press
in the UK and in certain other countries

First published 1995
This edition 2005

British Library Cataloguing in Publication Data
Data available

ISBN-13: 978-0-19-917958-9
ISBN-10: 0-19-917958-1

1 3 5 7 9 10 8 6 4 2

Available in packs
Stage 10 Pack of 6:
ISBN-13: 978-0-19-917954-1; ISBN-10: 0-19-917954-9
Stage 10 Class Pack:
ISBN-13: 978-0-19-917960-2; ISBN-10: 0-19-917960-3
Guided Reading Cards also available:
ISBN-13: 978-0-19-917962-6; ISBN-10: 0-19-917962-X

Cover artwork by Joseph Sharples
Photograph of John Coldwell © Caroline Scott Photography, Staplehurst

Printed in China by Imago

There was a problem at the castle.

'I give up,' said Mrs Binns, the royal cleaner, 'There's too much work here for one person.'

Mrs Binns gave Queen Norah the keys to the castle and left.

Queen Norah told the rest of the
royal family.

'What are we going to do?' asked
Princess Jane.

'For a start, you cannot have your
friends round here any more,' said
Queen Norah.

'Why not?' asked Princess Jane.

'Because they make too much mess.'

'Perhaps we can all try to keep the castle tidy,' said King Harry. 'I'm sure that Captain Jones and Captain Smith will help. I can even do a bit of washing myself.'

'What!' shouted Queen Norah. 'People will say that King Harry does his own cleaning! Never!'

'We can put up an advert for a cleaner,' said Princess Jane.

'Good idea,' said Queen Norah. 'Write an advert at once.'

Princess Jane wrote a notice.

She pinned it to the castle door.

Cleaner wanted
Good Pay
Ask at the Castle

The days went by and nobody
came to ask about the cleaning job.
The castle became dirtier and dirtier.
There were no more clean clothes
and no more clean plates.

One morning Queen Norah heard
singing coming from the kitchen. She
popped her head round the door. She
saw a shocking sight.

King Harry was at the sink
doing the dishes. Captain Smith
was mopping the floor. Captain
Jones was washing the royal shirts.

'Stop this at once,' cried Queen Norah.

'These are not jobs for a king and his captains. You should be out fighting dragons.'

'We've never seen any dragons, dear,' said the King.

'You have never even looked for them,' said Queen Norah.

Queen Norah was so upset that she made up her mind to go on a royal tour that minute. 'And you three: don't even think about doing the cleaning.' She added, 'You will go on a quest while I'm away.'

'A quest?' said King Harry. He went pale. 'A quest for dragons?'

'You can look for them, too,' said
Queen Norah. 'But the main job is to
find a new cleaner.'

'What about me?' asked Princess
Jane.

'You can stay at home. And don't let
any burglars in. Or your friends.'

Queen Norah sent for her royal cases
and bags and began her royal tour.

King Harry, Captain Jones and
Captain Smith set off on their quest for
a cleaner. They looked very unhappy.

Princess Jane waved them goodbye.

'It's not fair,' sniffed Princess Jane.
'Everyone's off on quests and tours, and
I am stuck on my own in this smelly
old castle.'

2

Princess Jane stuck out her lip and had a good sulk.

She had just finished her sulk when there was a knock on the castle door.

Princess Jane opened the door. There stood three figures in masks.

'We are the Masked Cleaning Ladies of Om,' said one.

'We were sent by your father, King Harry,' said another.

'That was quick,' said Princess Jane. 'Where is my father?'

'Chasing dragons,' said the third masked figure.

'Why are you masked?' asked
Princess Jane.

'We have to protect ourselves from
the dust,' said one. 'Can we start?'

All day the Masked Cleaning Ladies
scrubbed, dusted, washed, and polished.
By evening, the castle sparkled.

'Now that the castle is clean you can
take off your masks,' said Princess Jane.

'Oh, no,' said one. 'We can't do
that.'

'Why not?' demanded Princess Jane.

'Er, er,' said another. 'If we take off
our masks we won't be the Masked
Cleaning Ladies of Om.'

Princess Jane began
to think very hard. Burglars
often wore masks. Queen Norah
had told her not to let burglars into
the castle.

The next day Princess Jane set out
to find out who the Masked Cleaning
Ladies really were.

The first Masked Cleaning Lady was
in the kitchen, stuffing a pile of dirty
shirts into the washing machine.

'Hm,' she said. 'Shall I wash this
tablecloth on "Hot" or "Very hot"?'

Princess Jane came up behind her.
She grabbed the tablecloth and pulled
it over the cleaning lady's head.

'Help!' mumbled the cleaning lady.
'Where am I?'

The second Masked Cleaning Lady
was scrubbing the dungeon floors.

'Excuse me,' said Princess Jane,
standing outside one of the cells.
'But it's very dirty in here.'

'I swept it only five minutes ago,' said the second cleaning lady. 'Let me have a look.'

She walked into the cell.

Princess Jane closed the door and turned the key.

The third cleaning lady was making
a terrific noise with the vacuum
cleaner. She did not see Princess Jane
creeping up behind her. Princess Jane
grabbed the vacuum. She pointed the
nozzle at the cleaning lady.

'One false move,' shouted
Princess Jane, 'and I'll suck you into
the vacuum. Now. Take off your mask.'

Slowly the cleaning lady took off
her mask.

'Father!' cried Princess Jane.

The other two cleaning ladies turned
out to be Captain Smith and Captain
Jones.

3

'I think that you had better explain,' said Princess Jane.

'Well,' said King Harry, 'we set off on our quest. When we reached the woods, we saw a dragon.'

'We *think* we saw a dragon,' said
Captain Jones.

'At least, we heard something
moving in the woods and it sounded
like a dragon,' said Captain Smith.

'So we thought we had better come
home,' said Captain Jones.

'We dressed up as cleaners,' said
Captain Smith.

'We rather like doing housework,' said King Harry. 'We like the smell of polish.'

'We like the hum of the vacuum cleaner,' said Captain Jones.

'We like the feel of soap flakes,' said Captain Smith.

'And it's much less dangerous than fighting dragons,' added King Harry.

'Dragons are very rare,' said Captain Jones. 'It's not fair to hunt them.'

'Hm,' said Princess Jane. 'It seems to me that you three have been telling lies. Father, you have always told me to tell the truth.'

'I'm very sorry,' said King Harry.

'What will the Queen say? She'll find out that you haven't found any cleaners or fought any dragons,' said Princess Jane. 'She'll send you on a year's dragon quest.'

King Harry, Captain Smith
and Captain Jones went pale.

'Please don't tell,' they begged.

'I won't tell if…' said Princess Jane.

'If what?'

'If my friends can come round to play.'

'Agreed,' said King Harry.

The next day, Queen Norah came back from her royal tour. She was very pleased to find the castle neat and tidy.

'So,' she said. 'The quest was a success. Who did you find?'

'We found three cleaners,' said King Harry.

'They wear masks,' said Captain Jones.

'And they can only come on Mondays,' said Captain Smith.

'Why's that?' asked Queen Norah.

'They are having lots of trouble with dragons,' said Princess Jane. 'Father and the captains are going to fight the dragons every Monday while the cleaners come and tidy the castle.'

'Harry,' said Queen Norah, 'I am so proud of you.'

'Now that we have proper cleaners,' said King Harry, 'don't you think that Jane's friends can come here again?'

Queen Norah was so pleased to be in a nice clean castle that she agreed at once.

Every Monday Queen Norah waves goodbye to King Harry and his two captains as they set off to fight dragons. Princess Jane's friends come to play. Later, the Masked Cleaning Ladies of Om arrive to clean the castle. So everybody is happy.

About the author

I was born in London in 1950 and now live by the seaside, in Ramsgate. In the evening I like to write stories and poems. I do this very quietly. Then I go downstairs and play jazz records very loudly. My family think that I do two very daft things. One is going up the garden every night looking for frogs, newts and hedgehogs. The other is supporting Gillingham Football Club.